London: 74
Fascinating Facts For
Kids

Richard Hanson

This book is just one of a series of "Fascinating Facts For Kids" books. For more fascinating facts about people, history, animals, and much more please visit:

www.fascinatingfactsforkids.com

Contents

Introducing London

1. London is the capital city of England and is situated in the southeast corner of the United Kingdom. It stands on the River Thames, which at 215 miles (346 km) in length is the longest river in England.

2. The history of London stretches back 2,000 years to when the Romans invaded Britain. It has grown into a city with a population of nearly nine million, making it the largest city in the United Kingdom.

3. London has a land area of more than 600 square miles (1,580 sq km) which is divided into thirty-two boroughs, each governed by its own local council.

The London Boroughs

4. London is home to some of the most famous buildings and landmarks in the world, including the Tower of London, St. Paul's Cathedral, the Houses of Parliament, and Tower Bridge.

St. Paul's Cathedral

History

5. When the Romans invaded Britain in the first century they built a bridge over the Thames and settled on the north bank of the river. The settlement soon grew into a town which the Romans called "Londinium."

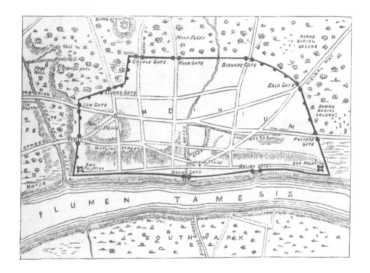

Londinium

6. London soon became a busy port, with ships arriving from mainland Europe carrying goods and people from all parts of the Roman Empire. London was soon a bustling and prosperous town with a population of around 20,000 people.

7. When the Romans left Britain in the fifth century London fell into decline, but after the

Norman Conquest of 1066 William the Conqueror made it the capital of England. Castles, a palace, and a cathedral were built and London began to thrive again.

William the Conqueror

8. By the Middle Ages London had become one of the largest cities in the world. As the population exploded, the streets became crowded and filthy, and people were forced to live in squalid conditions in tightly-packed houses.

9. The overcrowded, dirty streets and houses provided the perfect home for rats. The fleas which lived in the coats of the rats were responsible for the spread of a dreadful disease known as "bubonic plague."

10. An outbreak of bubonic plague started in the spring of 1665, and spread rapidly through the population. By August, 7,000 people a week were dying from the plague, and a total of 100,000 lives were lost before the disease died out during the cold winter months.

Bodies being taken away for burial

11. The year after the plague, another disaster struck London. In the early hours of September 2, 1666, a bakery in Pudding Lane caught fire. Strong winds swept the flames across the narrow streets, setting fire to the city's wooden buildings, until soon the whole of London was ablaze.

London ablaze

12. After five days the wind dropped and the Great Fire of London came to an end. Thousands of people had been made homeless and the city was destroyed. Remarkably, only nine people lost their lives.

13. The city was quickly rebuilt after the fire. To prevent such a catastrophe happening again, the old wooden houses were replaced by brick buildings, and the streets were made wider.

14. The eighteenth and nineteenth centuries saw a growth of trade and industry that made London the biggest and richest city in the world. The city expanded further with the arrival of the railways, which meant that people could live in the suburbs and travel into London every day for their work.

15. During World War Two much of London was again destroyed. Night after night hundreds of aircraft flew from Germany to drop their bombs on the city below. By the time the air raids stopped, 20,000 Londoners had been killed and millions left without homes.

Firefighters after an air raid

16. Today, London is a blend of the old and new, with futuristic modern buildings standing beside historical buildings of the past. It is one of the most diverse cities on Earth - people from all over the planet have chosen to live there, and you can hear more languages spoken in London than in any other city in the world.

Old and new

Landmarks

The Tower of London

17.   Following the Norman Conquest in 1066, William the Conqueror spent the next twenty years building a huge fortress in the middle of London. It became known as the White Tower and at ninety feet (30 m) high, it was the tallest building in London. Future kings added more buildings, walls, and towers to eventually give us the Tower of London of the present day.

The Tower of London

18.   For centuries, the Tower was the most secure castle in England and many prisoners have been held in its dungeons. Kings and queens stored their valuables at the Tower, and even today the priceless Crown Jewels are housed there.

A part of the Crown Jewels

19. Dozens of executions have taken place at the Tower over the centuries, including the beheading of three queens - Anne Boleyn (1536), Catherine Howard (1542) and Lady Jane Grey (1554). The ghost of Anne Boleyn is one of many that are said to haunt the Tower.

Anne Boleyn

20. For more than 500 years the Tower has been guarded by the famous Yeoman Warders - or "Beefeaters." Around forty Beefeaters live and work there today, acting as tourist guides and performing ceremonial duties.

A Beefeater

21. A colony of ravens lives at the Tower. There is a legend that says if ever they leave the Tower then the kingdom will come to an end. Luckily, the ravens have all had their wings clipped so that flying and escaping is impossible!

The Tower ravens

The Houses of Parliament

22. The Houses of Parliament, also known as the Palace of Westminster, is the home of the House of Commons and the House of Lords. Elected Members of Parliament ("MPs" for short) sit in the House of Commons representing the people of the United Kingdom. The House of Lords is made up of unelected members and helps with the passing of laws and checking the work of the Government.

23. Following the destruction of the original Palace of Westminster in a fire in 1834, it was decided to construct a new building. It was to be built in the "Gothic" style - an ornate type of architecture popular in the Middle Ages - and following more than thirty years of design and construction, the new 1,100 room Houses of Parliament was completed in 1870.

The Palace of Westminster

24. The most famous part of the Houses of Parliament is the 316-feet-high (96 m) clock tower, known as the Elizabeth Tower. Behind the clock at the top of the tower is a massive fifteen-ton (13,760 kg) bell, known as Big Ben. Four smaller bells chime at 15, 30 and 45 minutes past the hour and the deep sound of Big Ben is heard on the hour.

The Elizabeth Tower

25. In the House of Commons, the Government MPs sit on one side of the chamber facing the Opposition MPs on the other. The two sides are separated by two red lines on the floor over which MPs are not allowed to tread. The lines are thirteen feet (3.96 m) apart - equivalent to two sword-lengths - so opposing MPs are encouraged to debate rather than fight!

Buckingham Palace

26. Buckingham Palace is the official London residence of the British Royal Family. It was originally a house owned by the Duke of Buckingham before being converted into a palace in the early nineteenth century. The first monarch to live there was Queen Victoria when she came to the throne in 1837.

Queen Victoria

27. Buckingham Palace measures 355 feet (108 m) across the front, 395 feet (120 m) from front to back, and is 80 feet (24 m) high. It has 775 rooms including 240 bedrooms and 19 State Rooms.

Buckingham Palace

28. The majestic State Rooms are used for formal occasions, such as entertaining foreign dignitaries with lavish banquets. Hanging from the ceilings are magnificent chandeliers, and on the walls are valuable paintings from the Royal Collection, which is the largest private art collection in the world.

29. When important guests visit Buckingham Palace for a royal banquet it can take three days to get the massive banqueting table ready. Each guest is allocated a space of 16½ inches (42 cm) and thousands of pieces of cutlery and glasses are needed for the many different courses to eat and wines to drink.

30. Buckingham Palace is a working building doubling as an office and home for the Royal Family. Around 300 people work at the palace and over 50,000 guests visit each year for state visits, royal ceremonies, and garden parties. During the summer months, when the Royal Family leave London, members of the public are allowed to explore the magnificent State Rooms.

Westminster Abbey

31. In the middle of the eleventh century the reigning English king, Edward the Confessor, ordered the building of a great church to stand beside his palace in Westminster. The result was Westminster Abbey, which has held the coronation of every British monarch since William the Conqueror in 1066.

32. The original church was replaced in 1245 when Henry III ordered the construction of a magnificent new abbey in the ornate and spectacular Gothic style. The present-day building is little changed from the abbey of King Henry's day.

Westminster Abbey

33. Since the time of Edward the Confessor, many kings and queens of England have been buried in Westminster Abbey. From the seventeenth century, important national figures were also buried there, and it has become a great honor to be buried or commemorated in the abbey.

34. Important non-royals to be buried at Westminster Abbey include scientists Isaac Newton and Charles Darwin, writers Charles Dickens and Rudyard Kipling, and composers George Frederick Handel and Henry Purcell. The only person to be buried in an upright position is the poet and playwright Ben Jonson.

Charles Darwin

Charles Dickens

Trafalgar Square

35. Trafalgar Square is a spacious public square built to commemorate the Battle of Trafalgar in 1805. The battle saw the British Navy, under the command of Admiral Lord Nelson, defeat the combined French and Spanish fleets in one of the greatest sea battles in history.

Trafalgar Square

36. In the middle of Trafalgar Square is a great monument to Lord Nelson. Designed in the architectural style of the ancient Greeks and Romans, Nelson's Column stands 169 feet (52 m) tall. Standing at the top of the column is an 18-feet-high (5.5 m) statue of Nelson.

Lord Nelson

37. Surrounding the base of Nelson's Column are the bronze statues of four lions. They were designed and made by the Victorian artist, Sir Edwin Landseer, who used a real dead lion to model his statues on. There are subtle differences on the faces and manes of the lions, and it is said that they will spring to life if Big Ben strikes thirteen.

38. Every year since 1947, the people of Norway have sent a 65-feet-high (20 m) Christmas tree to Britain, to be placed in Trafalgar Square in recognition of the help the British gave to Norway during World War Two. It is erected twelve days before Christmas and decorated with 500 lights. It is on display until twelve days after Christmas when it is taken away for recycling.

Norway's Christmas tree

Tower Bridge

39. Tower Bridge is the only bridge across the Thames that can be raised to allow large vessels to sail past it. Huge powerful engines are used to raise two sections of the bridge, taking just over a minute to do so.

Tower Bridge

40. Tower Bridge was built in the late nineteenth century by more than 400 workers and at a cost of £1,184,000 (around £120 million in today's money). The finished bridge was 800 feet (244 m) wide, with a 213-feet-high (65 m) tower on each side. The central span between the towers is 200 feet (61 m).

41. In its first year of opening Tower Bridge was raised more than 6,000 times, but with less river traffic these days it might be raised only two or three times a day - good news for the thousands of motorists who cross the bridge every day.

Art & Culture

42. London is home to some of the world's great museums and art galleries, including the British Museum which opened in 1753 and is the oldest museum in the world.

The British Museum

43. The British Museum has over eight million objects, which chart the history of the world from the Stone Age right up to the twentieth century. Only one percent of the collection (80,000 objects) is on display, and it includes the finest examples of Egyptian antiquities outside of Egypt itself.

44. The Natural History Museum has a huge range of exhibits from the natural world and is famous for its collection of dinosaur skeletons. For years a replica of an 85-feet-long (26 m)

Diplodocus - known as "Dippy" - was on display in the museum's main hall. It was replaced in 2017 by a blue whale skeleton, before being taken on a two-year tour of the United Kingdom.

"Dippy"

45. The Science Museum is packed with over 300,000 objects from the world of science and technology. The exhibits include the oldest surviving steam locomotive, the first ever jet engine, and some of the earliest computers. Part of the museum is dedicated to flight and on display is the Command Module of Apollo 10, which flew round the Moon in May 1969, two months before the first Moon landing.

Apollo 10's Command Module

46. The National Gallery is situated on the north side of Trafalgar Square and it houses one of the world's greatest collections of paintings, which includes masterpieces by artists such as Van Gogh, Monet, Rembrandt, and Michelangelo.

The National Gallery

47. When the National Gallery first opened in 1831, there was a commitment that art should not be the exclusive privilege of the rich. Its situation in the center of London meant that wealthy people could reach it easily in their carriages from the west, and poor people could get there by foot from the east, ensuring the paintings could be seen and enjoyed by all classes of society.

48. London is home to two world famous opera houses - the Royal Opera House and the London Coliseum. The Coliseum is the largest theater in London with 2,359 seats, and the Royal Opera House is the third largest with a capacity of 2,256.

49. The Royal Opera House and the London Coliseum are also the home of world-renowned ballet companies. The Royal Ballet dances at the Royal Opera House, and the English National Ballet performs at the Coliseum.

50. London has a rich classical music heritage and is the home of five of the world's great symphony orchestras - The London Symphony Orchestra, The London Philharmonic Orchestra, The Royal Philharmonic Orchestra, the Philharmonia Orchestra, and the BBC Symphony Orchestra.

51. There are many other smaller orchestras and groups that are based in London including the London Sinfonietta, which specializes in modern classical music, and the Orchestra of the Age of Enlightenment, which plays on old instruments so that the music sounds just like it did when it was first written.

52. One of the newest theaters in London is Shakespeare's Globe Theatre, which opened in 1997. It was built as an almost exact copy of Shakespeare's original 16th-century theater. The new Globe had to get special permission to have a thatched roof - it has been illegal for any building in London to have a thatched roof ever since the Great Fire of 1666.

Shakespeare's Globe Theatre

53. Every summer an eight-week-long festival of classical music takes place in London. The "Promenade Concerts," which began in 1895, are commonly known as "The Proms," and take place mainly at the Royal Albert Hall - a massive circular shaped concert hall in South Kensington.

The Royal Albert Hall

54. The Proms attract all the world's top orchestras and musicians who play in front of audiences of over 5,000. The festival ends with the famous "Last Night of the Proms" - a light-hearted concert that celebrates British tradition with patriotic music.

Sport & Entertainment

55. Wembley Stadium in northwest London is Europe's second largest soccer stadium with a crowd capacity of 90,000. When its sliding roof is in place it becomes the largest covered stadium in the world. The England soccer team play all their home games at Wembley and the stadium stages the world-famous FA Cup Final every May.

Inside Wembley Stadium

56. Wembley Stadium was opened in 2007, replacing the old stadium which had stood since 1934. The most striking feature of the new stadium is the huge arch that spans the length of the roof. It stretches 1,033 feet (315 m) from end to end and rises 440 feet (134 m) above the ground, making it visible from miles around.

The Wembley Arch

57. Every summer, in the south London suburb of Wimbledon, one of the world's major tennis tournaments takes place. The first Wimbledon took place in 1877, making it the oldest tennis tournament in the world. The first Wimbledon final attracted a crowd of just 200 people, but nowadays it is watched by 15,000 spectators as well as a global TV audience of millions.

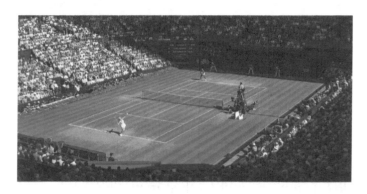

Wimbledon's Centre Court

58. England's national summer game of cricket is played at two grounds in London - Lord's Cricket Ground and The Oval. Middlesex play at Lord's and Surrey play at The Oval. The England cricket team also play international matches at the two grounds, attracting large crowds for the five-day-long games.

Cricket at Lord's

59. Twickenham Stadium, in southwest London, is the home of English Rugby Union. Its 82,000 capacity makes it the second largest stadium in the UK and the largest rugby stadium in the world. Before the first game was played there in 1909, Twickenham was used for growing vegetables and even today it is affectionately known as "The Cabbage Patch."

60. The London Marathon has been held every spring since 1981, inspired by the popularity of the annual New York marathon, which first took place in 1970. The first race attracted nearly 7,000 runners, and nowadays around 40,000 people try to complete the 26.2-mile (42km) course, raising huge sums of money for charity.

London Marathon runners

61. The West End of London is one of the most famous theater districts in the world. The thirty-eight theaters of the West End attract millions of visitors from all over the world every year to watch the many plays and musicals on offer.

62. The West End is the home of the world's longest-running play – "The Mousetrap," by Agatha Christie - which opened in 1952. It is a murder mystery and after every performance the audience is asked to never reveal the identity of the murderer.

63. The oldest theater in the West End is the Theatre Royal, Drury Lane, which was built in 1663. It is said to be the most haunted theater in London. One of the many ghosts is said to push actors into better positions on the stage and to give them a pat on the back if they perform well!

Theatre Royal, Drury Lane

Getting Around

64. London is world-famous for its bright red double-decker buses. The classic "Routemaster" was replaced in 2005 by more modern buses, although some can still be seen on the streets of London, full of tourists on sight-seeing trips.

A classic Routemaster

65. The London bus wasn't always red. Before 1907 lots of different companies ran buses of many different colors. The London General Omnibus Company decided to paint its buses red to make them stand out from their rivals and they soon became the biggest bus operator in the city.

66. There are around 8,500 buses in London serving 700 different routes and stopping at 19,000 bus stops. The longest bus route is the X26 which covers the twenty-four miles (39 km) from Croydon to Heathrow, a journey that can take up to two hours.

67. London's taxicabs are almost as well-known as the red buses. Traditionally black, London's 21,000 taxis can these days be seen in a range of colors with many carrying advertising.

A London taxi

68. Anyone who applies to become a London cab driver has to memorize the 25,000 streets, 320 routes, and the hundreds of landmarks within a
six-mile (10 km) radius of Charing Cross, the official center of London. It can take up to four years to learn all this information and only around half the applicants are successful.

69. The London Underground opened in 1863 when the world's first underground train made its 3½-mile (6 km) journey from Paddington Station to Farringdon. Today the underground network - or the "Tube," as it is affectionately known - has grown to 250 miles (400 km) of track, although less than half that distance is actually underground.

A London tube train

70. The eleven lines of the underground network - Bakerloo, Central, Circle, District, Hammersmith & City, Jubilee, Metropolitan, Northern, Piccadilly, Victoria, and Waterloo & City - are served by 270 stations and five million passengers travel on the Tube every day.

Assorted London Facts

71. The Great Fire of London is commemorated by The Monument, the tallest individual stone column in the world. Its height of 202 feet (61 m) is the exact distance from The Monument to the site of the bakery where the fire started.

The Monument

72. London's tallest building is "The Shard," which has a height of 1,016 feet (310 m) and is one of the tallest skyscrapers in Europe. Visitors to the viewing gallery on the 72nd floor can experience a 360°, 40-mile (65 km) view of London and beyond.

The Shard

73. Every August the biggest street party in Europe takes place in West London. The Notting Hill Carnival is a celebration of London's Caribbean community, and attracts hundreds of thousands of visitors to London to see the colorful parades and enjoy the Caribbean culture. The first carnival in 1966 attracted around 500 people but these days as many as two million visitors can be expected on the streets of Notting Hill.

Notting Hill Carnival

74. People have been coming to live and work in London for hundreds of years, and many famous men and women are celebrated with a "Blue Plaque," which is a sign attached to the building where the person lived or worked. There are over 900 Blue Plaques on buildings across London honoring the people who lived or worked there.

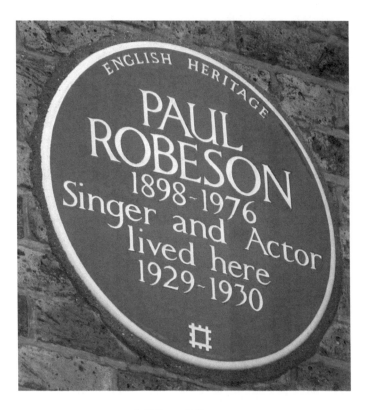

A Blue Plaque

Illustration Attributions

The London Boroughs
Notscott [CC BY-SA 3.0
(https://creativecommons.org/licenses/bysa/
3.)] modified

Londinium
Fremantleboy, Drallim (translation) [CC BY 2.5
(https://creativecommons.org/licenses/by/2.5)]modified

William the Conqueror
National Portrait Gallery, London [1] [Public domain]
{{PD-US}}

Bodies being taken away for burial
unknown [Public domain]
{{PD-US}}

London ablaze
Yale Center for British Art [Public domain]

Firefighters after an air raid
New York Times Paris Bureau Collection [Public domain]

A part of the Crown Jewels
United Kingdom Government [Public domain]

Anne Boleyn
[Public domain]
{{PD-US}}
A Beefeater
Nelly1974 [CC BY-SA 3.0
(https://creativecommons.org/licenses/by-sa/3.0)]

The Tower ravens
ingo zwank (iz) [CC BY-SA 3.0
(http://creativecommons.org/licenses/by-sa/3.0/)]

The Palace of Westminster
Adrian Pingstone (talk • contribs) [Public domain]

Queen Victoria
Friedenstein Castle [Public domain]
{{PD-US}}

Charles Darwin
Elliot & Fry
{{PD-US}}

Charles Dickens
unattributed [Public domain]
{{PD-US}}

Trafalgar Square
Christian Reimer [CC BY-SA 2.0
(https://creativecommons.org/licenses/by-sa/2.0)]

Lord Nelson
RedCoat [CC BY-SA 4.0
(https://creativecommons.org/licenses/by-sa/4.0)]

Norway's Christmas tree
Laura Bittner [CC BY 2.0
(https://creativecommons.org/licenses/by/2.0)]

The British Museum
Ham [CC BY-SA 3.0
(http://creativecommons.org/licenses/by-sa/3.0/)]

"Dippy"
08pateldan [CC BY-SA 3.0
(https://creativecommons.org/licenses/by-sa/3.0)]

Apollo 10's Command Module
Bruno Barral (ByB)The original uploader was ByB at
French Wikipedia. [CC BY-SA 2.5
(https://creativecommons.org/licenses/by-sa/2.5)]

Made in United States
Troutdale, OR
11/04/2024

24426864R00037